THE
PEANUT BUTTER
COOKBOOK
From Soup to Nuts with
America's Favorite Spread

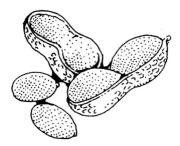

Judi & Tony Meisel
Photographs by Lionel Martinez

SMITHMARK

This edition published in 1993 by
SMITHMARK Publishers Inc.
16 East 32nd Street, New York, NY 10016

SMITHMARK books are available for bulk purchase
for sales promotion and premium use.
For details write or call the manager of special sales,
SMITHMARK Publishers Inc.,
16 East 32nd Street, New York, NY 10016; 212-532-6600.

Produced by AM Publishing Services
227 Park Avenue, Hoboken, NJ 07030
and
Wieser & Wieser, Inc.
118 East 25th Street, New York, NY 10010

Pottery courtesy of The Doofpot, Greenport, NY

Origination and Printing: Regent Publishing Services Ltd.

Printed in Hong Kong

10 9 8 7 6 5 4 3 2 1

ISBN 0-8317-7097-X

INTRODUCTION

The pleasures of eating supposedly get more sophisticated with age, yet certain foods retain their magic no matter what. Peanut butter—smooth or crunchy, commercial or homemade, organic or sugared and salted—is one of those foods. Everyone grew up with peanut butter and jelly sandwiches, unless they were castaways on some desert island. These were Mom's answer to a quick lunch or snack, along with a tall glass of cold milk. Familiar, unthreatening peanut butter was good for you, too.

It still is. Peanut butter contains large gobs of protein, polyunsaturates and minerals. True, it's high in fat, but it's vegetable fat and won't clog your arteries. It does stick to the roof of your mouth and between your teeth, but part of the fun is the challenge of vacuuming without having to brush your teeth.

Peanut butter traditionally has been thought of as kids' food. Adults, when they do eat it, get devious, sneaking a spoonful when no one is watching, spreading an apple slice with a surreptitious smear. You will really have to learn to modify your behavior—peanut butter is not a substance only for the mouths of little kids and unruly teenagers.

Peanut butter is good for many things other than as a spread for white bread. Both children and adults can relish it in appetizers, soups, sauces, main dishes, salads and desserts and confections. Its presence adds silkiness and a deeply satisfying, underlying taste to all it touches and combines with. *The Peanut Butter Cookbook* contains simple, easy-to-prepare, delicious recipes for expanding your peanut butter horizons.

Judi and Tony Meisel
New Suffolk, NY

Peanut butter topped with frizzled ham makes an appetizing snack.

MAKING PEANUT BUTTER

Making peanut butter from scratch may not be as easy as opening a jar, but it will not only taste fresher but will be free of additives, sugar, stabilizers and other not-so-good-for-you additions.

2 cups peanuts, either fresh or roasted
1–2 tablespoons peanut oil

You can use either freshly-shelled peanuts or roasted ones. Though you can buy roasted nuts from the market, making your own is fun and takes little time. Shell the peanuts and rub them between your hands to remove the papery covering. Spread them on a cookie sheet in one layer and place in a 300 degree oven for 15 minutes or until lightly browned. Let cool and proceed.

You can use either a food processor or a blender for making peanut butter. The processor is both faster and more likely to produce and evenly textured product. Place the peanuts in the processor container and give it a few short bursts to pulverize the peanuts. Slowly start adding the oil until you have reached the thickness and consistency you desire. A short processing time will give you chunky peanut butter. A long processing—over 1 minute— will provide smooth peanut butter.

The peanut butter will keep for a long time refrigerated and only slightly less on the cupboard shelf. It's a good idea to make it as you need it, since all nut butters will deteriorate in flavor over time. The oil you added, as well as the natural oils in the peanuts, may separate over time. Either whisk them back into the emulsion or drain the peanut butter for a slightly lower-fat snack.

PEANUT BUTTER SANDWICHES

Though this sounds like an exercise in the ordinary, peanut butter can be used in all sorts of unusual and delicious sandwiches. Try some of the variations following:

PEANUT-ONION SANDWICHES
Spread thinly sliced pumpernickel with hot mustard, then with peanut butter. Top with finely-sliced sweet onions that have been soaked in cold water for an hour, then dried. Top with another slice of pumpernickel.

PEANUT-HAM DELIGHTS
Spread split biscuits or cornbread with peanut butter. Top with sliced of frizzled ham and chutney. Heated in the oven for a few minutes, the flavor will deepen and improve.

PEANUT TORTILLAS
Spread peanut butter on warm tortillas, either corn or wheat, roll up and eat. Crumbled bacon can be added before rolling up.

PEANUT-SPROUTS
Spread whole wheat bread with peanut butter. Cover with fresh sprouts.

PEANUT-BACON
Spread slices of crusty peasant bread with peanut butter. Top with crisply fried bacon, or crumble the bacon on top and heat under the broiler for a few minutes.

PEANUT-WALNUT-CREAM CHEESE

Combine 1 cup smooth peanut butter with 1/4 cup chopped walnuts and 1 3-ounce package cream cheese. Spread on date-nut or raisin bread.

PEANUT-SARDINE

Spread rye bread with peanut butter. Top with skinned and boned sardines. A slice of onion is good with this.

PEANUT-CHICKEN

Spread good white bread with peanut butter. Top with slices of cooked chicken and top with a dollop of mayonnaise.

Peanut-cheese spread.

HOT CHILI-PEANUT BUTTER DIP

Use this as a snack or party dip.

1 onion, chopped
2 cloves garlic, chopped
1 tablespoon oil
1 1/2 cups peanut butter
1/2 cup canned chili peppers, chopped
white wine
1/4 cup parsley, chopped

Sauté the onion and garlic in the oil until soft and lightly browned. Add the peanut butter, chilies and enough white wine to make a thick dip and cook for 10 minutes on low heat. Stir in the parsley before serving with tortilla chips or crackers. Makes 2 cups.

PEANUT-CHEESE SPREAD

6 ounces sharp cheddar or jack cheese
3/4 cup smooth peanut butter
1 tablespoon vegetable oil
1/4 teaspoon Tabasco
pepper to taste
1/4 cup red wine or sherry

Cream all ingredients together with a fork or in a food processor. Pack in a bowl or ramekin and let stand at least 2 hours for flavors to meld. Serve with crackers or toast.

PEANUT SOUP

Peanut soup is a traditional Southern dish, most especially in Virginia. Most traditional recipes produce a thick, unctuous brew, more than a cup of which will fill you up beyond redemption. This version uses chunky peanut butter flavored with onions and cumin and is light enough to start a hot summer's day meal.

1 large Bermuda onion or 2 Vidalia onions, finely chopped
2 tablespoons sweet butter
1 teaspoon ground cumin
1/2 cup chunky peanut butter
4 cups hot chicken broth
1/2 teaspoon ground black pepper

Melt the butter in a medium saucepan over low heat. Add the chopped onion and cover. Cook as gently as possible for 125 minutes, until the onion is soft and golden, almost melted. Add the cumin and peanut butter and stir until smooth. Now, gradually add the chicken broth, stirring constantly, until a light, smooth mixture is achieved. Add the pepper and serve. Serves 4.

Variation: Garnish with a spoonful of lightly whipped cream mixed with finely minced chives.

JAVANESE PORK SATÉS

1/4 cup peanut butter
1 1/2 teaspoons ground coriander
1 teaspoon salt
1/2 teaspoon cayenne
1 teaspoon ground cumin
4 medium onions, chopped
freshly ground black pepper
2 cloves garlic, minced
1 1/2 tablespoons lemon juice
1 tablespoon brown sugar
3 tablespoons dark soy sauce
2 pounds boneless, pork, cut in 1 1/2-inch cubes

Mix together all ingredients except for the pork. Add pork cubes and mix together to coat all pieces thoroughly. Cover and refrigerate at least four hours. Thread meat on skewers and grill or broil for 20-25 minutes, turning frequently, and basting with any excess marinade, until crusty brown on all sides.

The meat can also be cut into smaller 3.4-inch cubes, threaded on smaller skewers, and served as an appetizer or as an accompaniment to drinks. Makes 6 servings as a main course or 12 servings as an appetizer.

PEANUT FRIED CHICKEN

Peanut butter adds a richness to the coating and helps retain the moisture in the chicken.

1 4 lb. chicken, cut into 8 pieces
1 cup crunchy peanut butter
1 cup unbleached flour
1/2 teaspoon salt
1 teaspoon freshly ground black pepper
oil or shortening for frying

Coat chicken pieces liberally and thoroughly with the peanut butter. Chill the chicken pieces for one hour. Meanwhile, combine the flour with the salt and pepper in a bowl. Remove the chicken from the refrigerator and roll each piece in the seasoned flour. As soon as all pieces are floured, place in a pan over medium heat containing oil or melted shortening to a depth of 1 inch. Fry approximately 25 minutes, turning the pieces several times, until they are golden all over and the juices of the thigh run clear when punctured. Note: the dark meat takes longer to cook than white, so you may either cook it first or use two pans. Serves 4 average eaters or 2 happy gluttons.

STEAK SANDWICHES
WITH PEANUT GLAZE

The traditional Philadelphia cheese steak is a godawful, gloppy mess, but delicious nevertheless. Here, a hot peanut topping replaces the cheese.

For each serving:
1 minute or sandwich steak
1 small onion, sliced
2 tablespoons oil
1 hard Italian roll

Heat the oil in a heavy skillet. Fry the onions until soft and lightly browned. Add the steak and cook over high heat for 2 minutes (any longer and it will; get tough). Shovel onto the roll and spoon on the peanut sauce.

For the sauce:
4 tablespoons peanut butter
1 teaspoon Worcestershire sauce
2 drops Tabasco or other hot sauce

Heat all ingredients in a small saucepan, stirring until well blended.

THAI NOODLES WITH PEANUT-GINGER SAUCE

This refreshing dish can be served as an appetizer or as part of an oriental buffet. The fish sauce and noodles can be bought in larger supermarkets and oriental shops.

8 ounce package of oriental rice noodles
1 tablespoon sesame oil
2 cloves garlic, finely chopped
1 green pepper, cored, seeded and julienned
1 red pepper, cored, seeded and julienned
2 scallions, coarsely chopped
1 tablespoon fresh ginger, julienned
4-6 ounces small, cooked shrimp
2 tablespoons nam phua (Thai fish sauce)
1 tablespoon soy sauce
1/4 cup smooth peanut butter

Place noodles in a large bowl and cover with boiling water for 5 minutes. In a saucepan, heat the sesame oil. Sauté the garlic, peppers, scallions, ginger and shrimp for 5-7 minutes over high heat, tossing constantly. Add the fish sauce, soy sauce and peanut butter and toss well. Drain the noodles well and place in a bowl. Pour the shrimp and vegetable mixture over and serve. Serves 4.

SPICY PEANUT-GARLIC ROAST PORK

A splendid entrée for a dinner party. Modern pork is lean and low in cholesterol.

1 3-pound boneless loin of pork, rolled and tied
2 cloves garlic, cut in slivers
1 tablespoon ground coriander
1 teaspoon black pepper

Glaze:
1/2 cup peanut butter
1 tablespoon brown sugar
1 teaspoon hot sauce
1 tablespoon mustard

With a sharp knife make incisions in the roast and insert cloves of garlic. Rub the meat with a mixture of coriander and pepper and let rest, at room temperature, for 1 hour. Place the roast on a rack in a roasting pan and cook in a 350 degree oven for 1 1/2 hours until just done (145 degrees on a meat thermometer). In the meantime, mix all the ingredients for the glaze, creaming well. Spread this over the roast after 1 1/2 hours cooking and return to the oven for 10 minutes at 450 degrees. The roast will acquire a rich, crunchy glaze. Serve with buttered noodles and steamed broccoli or green peas. Serves 6.

CHICKEN CURRY

Curry is a good, quick standby. Quick to make, subject to infinite variations, it makes a complete meal along with rice and chutney.

2 tablespoons butter
1 large onion, chopped
1 clove garlic, chopped
2 heaped tablespoons curry powder or paste
1 tart apple, cored and chopped
1 tablespoon fresh ginger, chopped
1/4 cup peanut butter
2 cups cooked chicken, cubed
1 1/2 cups chicken broth

Melt the butter in a saucepan over medium heat. Add the onion and garlic and cook until soft and translucent. Add the curry powder and paste, mix well and let cook for 2 minutes. Add the apple, ginger, peanut butter, chicken and broth and simmer for 15 minutes. Serve over rice with chutney, chopped peanuts, grated coconut and chopped scallions. Serves 4.

CHUNKY PEANUT BUTTER POTATO PANCAKES

1 pound potatoes, grated
1 onion grated
1/4 cup chunky peanut butter
1 egg, beaten
1/2 teaspoon black pepper
1/4 cup butter or shortening
applesauce

Peel and grate the potatoes by hand or in a food processor. Place in a bowl of cold water and rinse to get rid of excess starch. Drain and press out as much moisture as possible. Combine the potatoes with the onion, peanut butter, beaten egg and pepper. Mix well. Heat a griddle or large skillet over medium heat. Add the butter or shortening. Drop large spoonsful of the potato mixture into the pan, just as if you were making pancakes. When browned on one side, turn and cook until evenly browned, about 15-20 minutes. Drain on paper towels and serve with applesauce. The amount of peanut butter can be increased for richer-tasting pancakes. Serves 4.

MACARONI WITH PEANUT-CHEESE SAUCE

The old stand-by with a new twist!

1 pound macaroni
3 tablespoons butter
3 tablespoons flour
2 cups warm milk
1 cup grated cheddar cheese
1/2 cup chunky peanut butter
1/2 teaspoon ground nutmeg
1 teaspoon black pepper
2 teaspoons salt

Boil the macaroni in at least 4 quarts of salted water until just firm. Drain and set aside. In a saucepan over low heat, melt the butter. Stir in the flour and blend thoroughly. Let cook 2 minutes. Slowly add the warm milk, stirring constantly, until well blended. Add the cheese and peanut butter and continue stirring until the cheese is melted and the whole is smooth and thick. Place the macaroni in a deep, oven-proof casserole. Pour the cheese mixture over and fold in. Place in a 400 degree oven for 20 minutes until hot through and browned on top. Serves 4.

SPICY STRING BEANS

Any green vegetable—asparagus, sugar snap peas, greens, broccoli—can be dressed in this manner. It makes a change and a good first course.

1 1/2 pounds string beans
2 tablespoons sesame oil
2 cloves garlic, chopped
1/2 cup peanut butter
1/2 teaspoon Tabasco
1/4 cup light cream

Boil the string beans in 4 quarts of salted water until just crisp, about 8-10 minutes. Drain immediately and set aside. In a large saucepan, heat the sesame oil. Sauté the garlic for 2 minutes over medium heat. Add the peanut butter and Tabasco and blend well. Add the cream and just heat through. Now add the string beans to the pan and toss well to coat them and impregnate them with the flavors of the sauce. Turn out into a serving bowl. Serves 4.

PEANUT SLAW

Cole slaw is one of those dishes you either love or don't. There are as many recipes for it as there are cooks and following is one of our favorites.

1 small green cabbage, 2-3 pounds
1/2 cup scallions, chopped
1 cup plain yogurt
1/2 cup peanut butter
2 tablespoons canned hot peppers, chopped
salt and pepper to taste

Cut the cabbage in quarters. Cut out the tough central core. Shred the cabbage as finely as possible. Place in a bowl of cold water and rinse. Drain thoroughly, pressing out as much moisture as possible. Mix the scallions, yogurt, peanut butter and hot peppers together in a small bowl. Pour over the cabbage and toss well. Let stand to blend the flavors. Serves 8-10.

Variation: grated carrots add a nice touch of color and sweetness.

PEANUT POTATO SALAD

2 pounds new potatoes
1/4 cup grated onion
1/2 cup cooked peas
1/2 cup mayonnaise
1/2 cup peanut butter
2 tablespoons lemon juice
salt and pepper to taste
1/4 cup peanuts, chopped

Boil the potatoes until just done. Peel and slice into 1/4-inch rounds. Mix with the grated onion and peas. Separately mix the mayonnaise, peanut butter, lemon juice, salt and pepper. If too thick, thin with a little milk. Pour over the vegetable mixture and toss lightly. Top with chopped peanuts. Served 6-8.

PEANUT WAFFLES

This breakfast standby becomes a whole new dish when spread with peanut butter. To make the waffles even more sumptuous, add chopped peanuts to the batter. Accompanied by ham or sausage, it becomes a delicious brunch or lunch dish.

FRUIT SALAD,
PEANUT VINAIGRETTE

This salad can be served as a main dish for lunch or as a dessert after a heavy meal. It's delicious either way.

2 bananas, peeled and sliced
    1/4-inch thick
1 mango, peeled, seeded and cut into
    1/2-inch chunks
1 grapefruit, peeled and cut into
    sections
2 oranges, peeled and cut into sections
1/2 cup smooth peanut butter
1/2 cup vegetable oil
1/4 cup granulated sugar
juice of 2 lemons
1/2 teaspoon powdered ginger
1/2 teaspoon black pepper
1 tablespoon dark rum
1/2 cup chopped peanuts

Mix all the fruits together in a serving bowl and chill for 1 hour. Mix all the remaining ingredients, except the chopped peanuts, in a shaker jar or blender until smooth and syrupy in consistency. Let stand 1 hour for flavors to blend. Serve salad with dressing poured over and chopped peanuts sprinkled on top. Serves 6.

PEANUT CUSTARD

2 cups milk
1/4 cup sugar
1/8 teaspoon salt
3 whole eggs
1/2 cup smooth peanut butter
1/2 teaspoon vanilla extract
Hot, not, boiling water

Preheat oven to 300 to 325 degrees. Have ready a pan with 4 large ramekins or 6 small Pyrex dishes. In a medium sized bowl, blend together the milk, sugar and salt. Beat the eggs and add to the milk mixture. Add the peanut butter and vanilla and stir until smooth. When the mixture is smooth transfer it to the ramekins or small custard cups, do not fill the cups completely. Place the cups in a baking pan and fill with an inch or two of hot water. Bake for one hour or until a knife blade inserted near the edge comes out clean. Cool, before refrigerating.

PEANUT PIE

1 9-inch pie shell
3 eggs
1/2 cup sugar
2 cups milk
1/2 cup smooth peanut butter
1 teaspoon vanilla extract

Preheat the oven to 450 degrees. Build up a fluted rim on the pie crust and prick the crust with a fork. Bake it in the oven for 10 minutes. Remove the crust and set aside. Reduce over temperature to 325 degrees. In a large mixing bowl beat the eggs. Add the sugar, and salt. Combine the milk and the peanut butter in a separate bowl and mix until smooth., add to the egg mixture along with the vanilla extract.. Mix well. Note this custard should be cool when it is transferred to the pie crust, so you may wish to make it before baking the crust. Pour the custard into the prebaked crust and bake for 30 minutes or until just firm. Cool before serving

PEANUT BUTTER COOKIES

1/2 cup butter
1/3 cup packed brown sugar
1/3 cup granulated sugar
1 egg
1 cup chunky peanut butter
1/2 teaspoon salt
1/2 teaspoon vanilla extract
1 1/4 cups unbleached flour

Preheat oven to 375 degrees. Beat butter with wire whisk until soft. Gradually add the two sugars until blended and creamy in texture. Beat in the remaining ingredients except the flour. Sift the flour before measuring and then mix in. Let the dough rest for 10 minutes, then form into balls about 3/4-inch in diameter. Place the balls on a greased cookie sheet or Teflon-coated (ungreased) sheet. Flatten slightly with the back of a fork and bake 5-10 minutes, until golden brown. Remove from oven and let cool on racks before serving. Makes two dozen cookies.

PEANUT BRITTLE

1 1/2 cups granulated sugar
1 cup light brown sugar, firmly packed
1/2 cup light corn syrup
1/2 cup water
a pinch of salt
1/4 cup unsalted butter
1/2 cup chunky peanut butter
1 cup unsalted roasted peanuts

Combine the granulated sugar, brown sugar, corn syrup and water in a heavy, medium-sized saucepan. Cook, stirring until the sugar is dissolved. Cook, without stirring, until a little of the mixture dropped into cold water becomes very brittle (300 degrees on a candy thermometer). Remove from the heat. Add the salt, butter, peanut butter, baking soda and stir just until mixed. Add the nuts and turn into a shallow greased pan. Let it rest for a minute and then pull until thin. Allow to cool. When cold, break the brittle into pieces. Store in an air tight container..